11+
Verbal Reasoning
GL & Other Styles

WORKBOOK 3

Verbal Reasoning Technique

Dr Stephen C Curran
with Katrina MacKay
Edited by Andrea Richardson

This book belongs to

ae PUBLICATIONS

Accelerated Education Publications Ltd

Contents

9. Alphabet Work   **Pages**

1. Alphabetical Order   3-8
2. Alphabet Reasoning   8-10
3. Mixed Examples   10-11

10. More Codes

1. Transfer Codes   12-18
2. Plus and Minus Codes   18-21
3. Pattern Codes   22-23
4. Mixed Examples   23-24

11. Word Play

1. Crosswords   25-27
2. Words within Words   27-30
3. Mixed Examples   31

12. Word Manipulation

1. Adding or Subtracting Letters   32-35
2. Compound Words   36-39
3. Two Missing Letters   39-40
4. Word Chains   41-44
5. Rearranging Letters   45-48
6. Rhyming Words   48-50
7. Mixed Examples   50-51

13. Grouping

1. Identifying the Group   52-55
2. Size, Sequence or Position   55-56
3. Mixed Examples   57

14. Revision

1. Alphabet Work   58-59
2. More Codes   59
3. Word Play   60
4. Word Manipulation   60-61
5. Grouping   62

© 2015 Stephen Curran

Chapter Nine
ALPHABET WORK
1. Alphabetical Order

Learning to place words in **Alphabetical Order** improves knowledge of letter order in the alphabet, finding words at speed in the dictionary, and spelling skills.

a. Basic Sequences

Example: Write these words in alphabetical order:

whitewash   whistle   valley   whispering   valet

1. As **v** comes before **w** in the alphabet the words **valet** and **valley** come before all the words that begin with **w**.

2. The first three letters of **valet** and **valley** are the same so we must go by the fourth letter. The **e** in **val_e_t** comes before the **l** in **val_l_ey**, so **valet** precedes **valley**.

    The first two words in order are **valet** and **valley**.

3. As all the remaining words have the same first three letters, **whi**, we must go by the fourth letter. As the **s** in **whispering** and **whistle** come before the **t** in **whi_t_ewash** it means they must come first.

4. To determine which is first out of **whispering** and **whistle** the fifth letter must be considered. As **p** in **whispering** comes before **t** in **whis_t_le**, **whispering** must come before **whistle**. This only leaves **whitewash**, which must be last.

Answer: **valet   valley   whispering   whistle   whitewash**

A B C D E F G H I J K L M N O P Q R S T U V W X Y Z

Exercise 9: 1

Write these words in alphabetical order:

Record scores out of ten here

1) mutton   uncle   butter   indigo   drawn
_____ _____ _____ _____ _____

2) elect   elbow   dentist   elastic   density
_____ _____ _____ _____ _____

3) sandbag   sandal   sandbank   sandstone   sand
_____ _____ _____ _____ _____

4) category   catacomb   catapult   cataclysm   cater
_____ _____ _____ _____ _____

5) transcribe   transmit   transcript   transpire   translate
_____ _____ _____ _____ _____

6) illuminate   illegal   illumination   illustration   illiterate
_____ _____ _____ _____ _____

7) encyclopaedia   encrypt   encampment   encourage   encase
_____ _____ _____ _____ _____

8) promotion   prolific   propaganda   prosper   prominent
_____ _____ _____ _____ _____

© 2015 Stephen Curran

9) whoever   wholesome   whosoever   wholesale   whomever

_____   _____   _____   _____   _____

10) quicksand   quinoa   quicken   quintet   quilting

_____   _____   _____   _____   _____

b. Selecting an Ordered Word

This is an extension of Basic Sequences where the specific alphabetical order placement of the word must be given.

Example: If these words were placed in alphabetical order, underline the word that would come fourth:

nature   nitrogen   national   nutrition   nightmare

1. As all the words begin with **n** we go straight to the second letter. This means that **nature** and **national** come before all the other words. As **nature** and **national** both begin with **nat** we must go by the fourth letter. As the **i** in **nat*i*onal** comes before the **u** in **nat*u*re**, **national** comes first and **nature** comes second.

   The first two words in order are **national** and **nature**.

2. The next two words, **nitrogen** and **nightmare**, both begin with **ni** so these two words must come next. To determine which is first out of **nitrogen** and **nightmare** we must go to the third letter. As **g** in **nightmare** comes before **t** in **ni*t*rogen**, **nightmare** must take precedence over **nitrogen**. This only leaves **nutrition**, which must come last.

The next three words in order are **nightmare**, **nitrogen** and **nutrition**.

This is the complete alphabetical list:

national   nature   nightmare   nitrogen   nutrition

3. The fourth word in the list must now be selected. It is not always necessary to carry out all the steps as the requested word may be reached before all the words have been placed in alphabetical order.

Answer: The fourth word is **nitrogen**.

A B C D E F G H I J K L M N O P Q R S T U V W X Y Z

Exercise 9: 2a   Place the following words in alphabetical order and underline the requested word in the sequence:

1) 5th: lardon   lashing   laptop   larynx   lapse

2) 2nd: barrel   barracks   barracuda   barrier   barren

3) 4th: healthy   hearse   headache   heartless   hearth

4) 1st: pronoun   prone   pronounce   pronate   prong

5) 3rd: roughage   roughen   rough   roughly   rouge

c. Selecting a Backwards Word

In this type of Alphabetical Order question we must order the words beginning with the letter on the right of each word rather than the left (i.e. spelling the words backwards). This will mean the words are put in alphabetical order backwards.

A B C D E F G H I J K L M N O P Q R S T U V W X Y Z

Example: If these words were written backwards and then arranged in alphabetical order, underline the word that would come fifth:

compose   choose   propose   purpose   whose

1. When written backwards all the words begin with **eso** so we must begin with the fourth letter. As the **h** in w<u>h</u>ose comes before the **o** in ch<u>o</u>ose, **whose** comes before **choose**.

    The first two words in order are **whose** and **choose**.

2. The remaining words begin with **esop** so we must begin with the fifth letter. As the **m** in co<u>m</u>pose comes before the **o** in pr<u>o</u>pose, this means **compose** comes before **propose**. This only leaves **purpose**, which must come last.

    The next three words in order are **compose**, **propose** and **purpose**.

    This is the complete alphabetical list:

    whose   choose   compose   propose   purpose

3. The fifth word in the list must now be selected. It is not always necessary to carry out all the steps as the requested word may be reached before all the words have been placed in alphabetical order. As this question requires the fifth word all the steps must be carried out.

    Answer: The fifth word is **purpose**.

A B C D E F G H I J K L M N O P Q R S T U V W X Y Z

Exercise 9: 2b

If these words were written backwards and then arranged in alphabetical order, underline the requested word in the sequence:

Score

6) 3rd: seatbelt   default   dealt   rebuilt   spoilt

7) 4th: sweater   seawater   cheater   rainwater   beater

8) 1st: dispensing   licensing   condensing   cleansing   rinsing

9) 5th: thorough   plough   through   enough   although

10) 2nd: September   remember   clamber   December   chamber

2. Alphabet Reasoning

Alphabet Reasoning is a variation of the Logical Reasoning question type (Workbook 2), except it only ever involves questions about the alphabet. These questions are solved by firstly understanding what is being asked and then breaking down the task into simple logical steps that will lead to a correct answer.

A B C D E F G H I J K L M N O P Q R S T U V W X Y Z

Example: Use the alphabet above to help with the following question.

How many more consonants than vowels are in the word **PARTICULAR**?

1. Count the number of consonants in the word **PARTICULAR**.

There are six consonants – they are underlined: **PARTICULAR**.

2. Count the number of vowels in the word **PARTICULAR**. There are four vowels – they are underlined: **PARTICULAR**.

3. Subtract the vowels from the consonants, i.e. six minus four is two.

Answer: There are **two** more consonants than vowels in the word **PARTICULAR**.

A B C D E F G H I J K L M N O P Q R S T U V W X Y Z

Exercise 9: 3 Use the alphabet above to help answer the following questions:

1) What is the 23rd letter of the alphabet? _____

2) If all of the vowels were removed from the alphabet, which would be the new 17th letter? _____

3) Which letter appears most often in the word **INDECIPHERABLE**? _____

4) How many more consonants than vowels are in the word **IDIOSYNCRATIC**? _____

5) How many letters in the word **SNOWDROP** come in the first half of the alphabet? _____

6) Which letter appears twice in the word **INTERACTIVE**, three times in the word **CELEBRATE** and four times in the word **REPRESENTATIVE**? _____

7) Make a three-letter word from the letters which appear more than once in the word **RETENTIVITY**. _____

8) Write the five letters from the word **UNEMPLOYMENT** that do not appear consecutively in the word but do appear consecutively in the alphabet. _____

9) What position in the alphabet does the middle letter of the word **QUICKENED** occupy? _____

10) Make a word from the letters which appear more than once in the word **TRANSMISSION**. _____

3. Mixed Examples

A B C D E F G H I J K L M N O P Q R S T U V W X Y Z

Exercise 9: 4 Use the alphabet above to help answer the following questions:

Score

Write these words in alphabetical order:

1) recipient   rhetorical   rummage   rapport   rotate

   _____ _____ _____ _____ _____

2) genetics   generic   genius   general   gender

   _____ _____ _____ _____ _____

3) If these words were placed in alphabetical order, underline the word which would come fourth:

   quench   queen   quest   queue   question

A B C D E F G H I J K L M N O P Q R S T U V W X Y Z

4) If these words were placed in alphabetical order, underline the word which would come third:

    transcription   transmission   transformation   transaction   transporter

5) If these words were written backwards and then arranged in alphabetical order, underline the word which would come third:

    sentence   insistence   existence   competence   pretence

6) If these words were written backwards and then arranged in alphabetical order, underline the word which would come second:

    medication   vacation   vocation   dedication   fabrication

7) Which letter occurs the same distance from the end of the alphabet as the letter **G** does from the beginning? _____

8) How many more consonants than vowels does the word **SUBCONTINENTAL** have? _____

9) Write the five letters in the word **CELEBRATED** that do not appear consecutively in the word but do appear consecutively in the alphabet. _____

10) Which letter appears twice in the word **SOCIOCULTURAL**, twice in the word **LOLLIPOP** and three times in the word **METHODOLOGY**? _____

Chapter Ten
MORE CODES
1. Transfer Codes

Transfer Codes involve letters, numbers or symbols, but they are all solved using the same technique. The code is established by placing each word in a grid and writing in which letter, number or symbol of the code represents each letter of the word. Once we know what represents each letter we have deciphered the code and can apply it to find other words.

These questions can also occur the other way around where a group of jumbled letters, numbers or symbols is given and a word must be found from the grid. It just means the process is reversed.

They are called Transfer Codes because they involve substituting one element for another once the code has been deciphered.

a. Letter for Letter

In **Letter for Letter** Transfer Codes only words and jumbled letters are used to create the codes.

Example: In the following question the same code is used to find both answers. The letters **EWHZBA** stand for **NUMBER** and **JGRQIB** stands for **STAPLE**.

a) What does **RZAWQG** stand for?
b) What is the code for **LEARN**?

1. Write the code **EWHZBA** in a grid above the word **NUMBER**. We can see that **E** represents **N**, **W** represents **U**, and so on.

Code	E	W	H	Z	B	A
Word	N	U	M	B	E	R

2. Write the code **JGRQIB** in a grid above the word **STAPLE**. We can see that **J** represents **S**, **G** represents **T**, and so on.

Code	J	G	R	Q	I	B
Word	S	T	A	P	L	E

3. We now apply the code to find the answer to part a) What does **RZAWQG** stand for? If we move downwards from code to word on both grids we can see that **R** represents **A**, **Z** represents **B**, and so on.

Code	R	Z	A	W	Q	G
Word	A	B	R	U	P	T

   Answer: a) **RZAWQG** stands for **ABRUPT**.

4. In a similar way we can use the word to find the answer to part b) What is the code for **LEARN**? If we move upwards from word to code on both grids we can see that **L** is represented by **I**, **E** is represented by **B**, and so on.

Code	I	B	R	A	E
Word	L	E	A	R	N

   Answer: b) **LEARN** in code is **IBRAE**.

A B C D E F G H I J K L M N O P Q R S T U V W X Y Z

Exercise 10: 1   Answer the following questions:

1) If **SQFBP** stands for **NIGHT**, what does **PBQSF** stand for? _____

2) If **MOVGWC** stands for **ANTLER**, what does **GWMCOV** stand for? _____

3) If **XARHYJ** stands for **INSECT**, what is **NICEST** in code? _____

4) If **LZKBOUN** stands for **PRAISED**, what does **NUOLKBZ** stand for? _____

5) If **EZFKAPDQ** stands for **HUSTLING**, what is **SUNLIGHT** in code? _____

6) The code **ASZUC** stands for **NORTH** and **UPKH** stands for **TIME**.

   a) What does **KSAUC** stand for? _____
   b) What is the code for **TRIO**? _____

7) The code **YSBSOGSK** stands for **RECEIVED** and **PYXBLMYS** stands for **FRACTURE**.

   a) What does **SKMBXLOGS** stand for? _____
   b) What is the code for **ARRIVED**? _____

8) The code **VDTIWQD** stands for **BECAUSE** and **TGJGWZ** stands for **COLOUR**.

   a) What does **QDVITDGWQ** stand for? _____
   b) What is the code for **AEROSOL**? _____

A B C D E F G H I J K L M N O P Q R S T U V W X Y Z

9) The code **JPXXB** stands for **HOLLY** and **RCSYQLF** stands for **MUNDANE**.

   a) What does **RQSJPXF** stand for? _____

   b) What is the code for **LOYAL**? _____

10) The code **BCVJWPT** stands for **HARMONY** and **JCBWHCPT** stands for **MAHOGANY**.

   a) What does **BWJWPTJ** stand for? _____

   b) What is the code for **ANAGRAM**? _____

Score

b. Number for Letter

In **Number for Letter** Transfer Codes only words and numbers are used to create the codes.

Example: If **53672** stands for **GLARE**, what does **36752** stand for?

1. Write the code **53672** in a grid above the word **GLARE**. We can see that **5** represents **G**, **3** represents **L**, and so on.

Code	5	3	6	7	2
Word	G	L	A	R	E

2. We now apply the code to find the answer, which in this case will be an anagram of **GLARE**. If we move downwards from code to word on the grid we can see

that **3** represents **L**, **6** represents **A**, and so on. Therefore **36752** will give us the anagram **LARGE**.

Code	3	6	7	5	2
Word	L	A	R	G	E

Answer: **36752** stands for **LARGE**.

A B C D E F G H I J K L M N O P Q R S T U V W X Y Z

Exercise 10: 2a Answer the following questions:

1) If **73245** stands for **FIBRE**, what does **24357** stand for?

2) If **16942** stands for **LAYER**, what is **EARLY** in the same code?

3) If **857146** stands for **ADVERB**, what does **648715** stand for?

4) If **3295476** stands for **KITCHEN**, what is **THICKEN** in the same code?

5) If **81364529** stands for **MARCHING**, what does **64138529** stand for?

c. Symbol for Letter

In **Symbol for Letter** Transfer Codes only words and symbols are used to create the codes.

Example: In the following question %*£@# stands for **STOVE**. What does @£ *#% stand for?

1. Write the code **%*£@#** in a grid above the word **STOVE**. We can see that **%** represents **S**, ***** represents **T**, and so on.

Code	%	*	£	@	#
Word	S	T	O	V	E

2. We now apply the code to find the answer, which in this case will be an anagram of **STOVE**. If we move downwards from code to word on the grid we can see that **@** represents **V**, **£** represents **O**, and so on. Therefore **@£ *#%** will give us the anagram **VOTES**.

Code	@	£	*	#	%
Word	V	O	T	E	S

Answer: **@£ *#%** stands for **VOTES**.

A B C D E F G H I J K L M N O P Q R S T U V W X Y Z

Exercise 10: 2b Answer the following questions:

6) a) If **£*%@#** stands for **CANOE**, what does **@£#*%** stand for? _____

   b) What is the code for **CAN**, using the same code? _____

7) a) If **?+$%!** stands for **CHARM**, what does **!$%?+** stand for? _____

   b) What is the code for **ARM**, using the same code? _____

A B C D E F G H I J K L M N O P Q R S T U V W X Y Z

8) a) If £?#@£# stands for **EARNER**, what does @£?#£# stand for? _____

   b) What is the code for **ARE**, using the same code? _____

9) In the following question $&*£%#$? stands for **ROUNDERS**.

   a) What does %&#? stand for? _____

   b) What would **DRONES** be in the same code? _____

10) In the following question $%%*&&!@# stands for **ACCESSORY**.

    a) What does $%@!&& stand for? _____

    b) What would **ARCS** be in the same code? _____

2. Plus and Minus Codes
a. Number Codes

Transfer Plus and Minus Codes are a combination of Transfer Codes and simple Plus and Minus Codes, the latter of which were covered in Workbook 1. In a similar way to Number to Letter Transfer Codes they involve giving each letter in the alphabet a number. However, these numbers must be consecutive, starting with 1 at the beginning of the alphabet. Many questions only involve the Transfer Code element as indicated below:

1	2	3	4	5	6	7	8	9	10	11	12	13	14	15	16	17	18	19	20	21	22	23	24	25	26
A	B	C	D	E	F	G	H	I	J	K	L	M	N	O	P	Q	R	S	T	U	V	W	X	Y	Z

Questions can be further complicated by introducing a Plus or Minus Code in the numbering system. A Plus or Minus Code would be calculated by counting the difference between the code number and the original alphabet numbering.

Example: If **4 3 10 18** stands for **FELT**, what does **18 3 25 16 17** stand for?

1. Number the alphabet 1-26.

1	2	3	4	5	6	7	8	9	10	11	12	13	14	15	16	17	18	19	20	21	22	23	24	25	26
A	B	C	D	E	F	G	H	I	J	K	L	M	N	O	P	Q	R	S	T	U	V	W	X	Y	Z

2. Write the code **4 3 10 18** in a grid above the word **FELT**.

Code	4	3	10	18
Word	F	E	L	T

3. Work out the pattern for each letter by counting along the alphabet.

Code	4	3	10	18
Pattern	-2	-2	-2	-2
Word	F	E	L	T

4. The pattern from word to code is **-2**. In order to answer this question we need to reverse the pattern so that it applies to code to word. The pattern is now **+2**.

Code	18	3	25	16	17
Pattern	+2	+2	+2	+2	+2
Word	T	E	A	R	S

Answer: **18 3 25 16 17** stands for **TEARS**.

A B C D E F G H I J K L M N O P Q R S T U V W X Y Z

Exercise 10: 3a Answer the following questions:

1) If **25 4 17** stands for **VAN**, **4 21 6** stands for _____ .

2) If **13 26 26 1** stands for **REEF**, **26 17 26 9** stands for _____ .

3) If **ECHO** in code is **4 4 7 16**, what is **LOFT** in code? _____

4) If **5 1 5 15 9** stands for **AWAKE**, **14 25 13 7 3** stands for _____ .

5) If **STORY** in code is **21 18 17 16 1**, what is **TODAY** in code? _____

b. Number and Letter Codes

Number and Letter Codes combine Letter to Letter Plus and Minus Codes with Plus and Minus Number Codes.

Example: If **20 H 5 J 9 P 23** stands for **PLANETS**, what does **7 H 25 O 24 A 22** stand for?

1. Write the code **20 H 5 J 9 P 23** in a grid above the word **PLANETS**.

Code	20	H	5	J	9	P	23
Pattern	-4	+4	-4	+4	-4	+4	-4
Word	P	L	A	N	E	T	S

2. The numbers in the code have been shifted left by **-4**.

3. The letters in the code have been shifted right by **+4**.

4. It is now possible to use the pattern to find the word for **7 H 25 O 24 A 22**. The pattern remains the same as both examples move from code to word. **7** must stand for **C**, **H** for **L**, and so on as shown below:

Code	7	H	25	O	24	A	22
Pattern	-4	+4	-4	+4	-4	+4	-4
Word	C	L	U	S	T	E	R

Answer: **7 H 25 O 24 A 22** stands for **CLUSTER**.

A B C D E F G H I J K L M N O P Q R S T U V W X Y Z

Exercise 10: 3b Answer the following questions:

6) If **GROUP** in code is **9 T 17 W 18**, what is **UNDER** in code? _____

7) If **P 2 W 15 H** stands for **METRE**, **W 6 J 2 U** stands for _____ .

8) If **LENGTH** in code is **17 G 19 I 25 J**, what is **HALVES** in code? _____

9) If **25 M 14 U 13 F 11** stands for **FLUTTER**, **11 V 25 G 5 F 23** stands for _____ .

10) If **PANCAKE** in code is **U 11 S 13 F 21 J**, what is **KNUCKLE** in code? _____

Score

3. Pattern Codes

Pattern Codes involve identifying how a word has been changed or concealed within a group of letters. For example, a letter pattern of alphabetically sequential letters could have been added or the word could be hidden inside a sequence of letters.

Example: If **FAOBXC** stands for **FOX**, what does **AANBTC** stand for?

1. Compare the pattern code **FAOBXC** with the word **FOX** to see what has been added. The letters of the alphabet starting with **A** have been placed between the letters of **FOX**. To make this clearer these letters have been underlined in the pattern code **FAOBXC**. If the letters **A**, **B** and **C** are removed we are left with **FOX**.

2. Now apply the same rule to find the missing word. If we take the pattern code **AANBTC** and remove every other underlined alphabetically sequential letter, we are left with the word **ANT**.

Answer: **AANBTC** stands for **ANT**.

A B C D E F G H I J K L M N O P Q R S T U V W X Y Z

Exercise 10: 4 Answer the following questions:

1) If **AFBECD** stands for **FED**, **AABNCT** stands for _____ .

2) If **BBOWWL** stands for **BOWL**, **LLOOOP** stands for _____ .

3) If **ROCK** is written **RZOYCXKW**, **COIN** is written _____ .

4) If **PPAMM** stands for **MAP**, **WWOSS** stands for _____ .

5) If **EYES** is written **EFYZEFST**, **SINK** is written _____ .

6) If **JLAMDNEO** stands for **JADE**, **NLOMNNEO** stands for _____ .

7) If **INTO** is written **IINTTO**, **PAGE** is written _____ .

8) If **XTYAZNAGBO** stands for **TANGO**, **XEYXZTARBA** stands for _____ .

9) If **YYTRAPP** stands for **PARTY**, **LLLAMSS** stands for _____ .

10) If **LITRE** is written **LQIRTSRTE**, **IMAGE** is written _____ .

Score

4. Mixed Examples

A B C D E F G H I J K L M N O P Q R S T U V W X Y Z

Exercise 10: 5 Answer the following questions:

1) The code **IMIIPXJ** stands for **SESSION** and **MIGOVOLM** stands for **ESCAPADE**.

A B C D E F G H I J K L M N O P Q R S T U V W X Y Z

1) a) What does **GOJOVM** stand for? _____
   b) What is the code for **ASSASSIN**? _____

2) If **KRAOYMY** stands for **INFESTS**, what does **AKMROYY** stand for? _____

3) If **DVFXLAI** stands for **SECTION**, what is **NOTICES** in code? _____

4) If **734164** stands for **GREASE**, what does **173446** stand for? _____

5) If **924858** stands for **FEASTS**, what is **SAFEST** in code? _____

6) In the following question **+&*&£%#&** stands for **LEVERAGE**.

   a) What does **£&*&%+** stand for? _____
   b) What would **LARGE** be in the same code? _____

7) If **12 5 22 5 18** stands for **LEVER** then **5 24 9 19 20** stands for _____.

8) If **SYMBOL** in code is **19 25 13 2 15 12**, what is the code for **MODIFY**? _____

9) If **SHHOWWW** stands for **SHOW**, **RIINGGG** stands for _____.

10) If **STORK** is written **ZSYTXOWRVKU**, **SCRAP** is written _____.

Score

Chapter Eleven
WORD PLAY

Word Play questions do not require a knowledge of word meanings. Instead the questions are based on the formation of letters within each word. Questions may involve deciding where words fit into a particular grid or whether or not they contain a particular set of letters.

1. Crosswords

Crosswords simply require the placement of words in the correct space on a grid of nine squares.

Example: Fit the words listed below into the crossword. Words can only be placed in one position.

E	R	R
B	A	A
B	I	T

BIT
BAA
RAI
RAT
ERR

1. Look for the first word that will only fit in one position. There is only one word that begins with **E** so **ERR** must be placed at the top of the crossword.

E	R	R
B		
B		

2. As there are two words beginning with **R** and two words beginning with **B** it does not matter which is dealt with first. The next word that fits must be determined by trial and error. The first combination puts **RAT** in the

first column followed by **RAI** but this is incorrect, as **BTI** occurs in the last row of the crossword and this is not a word. If **RAI** is placed in the first column followed by **RAT**, both **BAA** and **BIT** also appear in the second and third rows.

E	R	R
B	A	A
B	T	I

Answer: The completed crossword is shown below.

E	R	R
B	A	A
B	I	T

Exercise 11: 1

Complete the crossword by fitting the five words horizontally or vertically into the grid:

1)

B		
I		
N		

BOW
NET
ORE
IRE
WET

2)

	R	
	Y	
	E	

CRY
TEN
CAT
YEN
AYE

3)

O	D	E

MEN
EON
DOE
ADO
DAM

4)

		G
		Y
		M

FIR
ICY
ICE
REM
FIG

5)

	K	
	E	
	Y	

THY
ASH
OAK
USE
OUT

6)

W	E	T

EVE
NET
PAN
PEW
AVE

7) [grid with S K Y in bottom row] ERA / MAY / YES / YAM / ARK

8) [grid with S E E in middle row] TEE / ACE / ICE / HAS / HIT

9) [grid: L E D / A G A / G O D] EGO / GOD / LAG / DAD / AGA

10) [grid with I / O / N in middle column] MUD / END / YOU / DYE / DIM

2. Words within Words

Looking for Words that Can or Cannot be Made from another word requires knowledge of the alphabet, reading ability and observational skills that can be sharpened with practice. The same technique of looking for Words that Cannot be Made is used for both of these exercises. This is because it is easier to spot something that should not be there rather than the other way round.

a. Words that Can be Made

Example: Underline the one word which can be made from the letters of the word in capital letters.

SEASONAL   lessons   allies   solos
              lawns   alone

1. Look for any double letters that should not be present. Remember **SEASONAL** does have two **A**s and two **S**s so this would be acceptable. However, **allies** has double **L** and **solos** has double **O** but **SEASONAL** only has one of each of these letters. Also, **lessons** has three **S**s. This means these words are eliminated.

SEASONAL ~~lessons~~ ~~allies~~ ~~solos~~ lawns alone

2. Now look for 'rogue' letters (letters that do not appear in **SEASONAL**). There is no **W** so **lawns** must be eliminated. This leaves **alone**, which must be the correct answer.

SEASONAL ~~lessons~~ ~~allies~~ ~~solos~~ ~~lawns~~ alone

3. Check against **SEASONAL** that **alone** has all the right letters. This confirms that **alone** is the correct answer and should be underlined.

Answer: **alone** can be made from the letters of the word **SEASONAL**.

Exercise 11: 2

Underline the one word which can be made from the letters of the word in capital letters:

1) **DISTRIBUTOR**   sibilant   budget   dribble   tourist   ruderal

2) **ABOLISHED**   bidding   sheath   disable   header   listen

3) **MULTIPLICATION**   politician   noisome   tunicate   canister   logistic

4) **CANTANKEROUS**   kerosene   tankard   ethnic   rotunda   aeronauts

5) **RESTORATION**   respite   trainers   narrative   Ionian   stared

6) **ENTOURAGE**   tongue   greater   turned   grunted   torment

7) **LONGEVITY**   gentle   violent   longest   voted   gloves

8) **CONUNDRUM**	mourned undone mound normal turn	
9) **KETTLEDRUM**	ruler demurely rudest leeks lurked	
10) **YACHTSMAN**	ache hymnal asthma nastily yarn	Score

b. Words that Cannot be Made

Example: Underline the one word which cannot be made from the letters of the word in capital letters.

INCIDENTAL   learnt ancient tinned canine dialect

It is simpler to look for the words that cannot be made as we only need to spot one word that has either double letters or 'rogue' letters that should not be there. The same technique is applied.

1. Look for any double letters that should not be present in any of the words. **INCIDENTAL** does have double **N** and double **I** so these do not count. The words **tinned**, **ancient** and **canine** also have double **N** and their other letters match **INCIDENTAL**. These three words can be eliminated.

INCIDENTAL   learnt ~~ancient~~ ~~tinned~~ ~~canine~~ dialect

2. Now look for rogue letters in the remaining two words **dialect** and **learnt**. There are no rogue letters in **dialect** as all its letters are found in **INCIDENTAL**. However, there is an **R** in **learnt** that does not appear in **INCIDENTAL**, which means **learnt** must be the correct answer and should be underlined.

Answer: **learnt** cannot be made from the letters of the word **INCIDENTAL**.

Exercise 11: 3 — Underline the one word which cannot be made from the letters of the word in capital letters:

Score

1) **ORCHESTRATE** — cheaters tractors racehorse shortest earshot

2) **WIDESPREAD** — despaired aspired spiders praise readied

3) **JOURNALISM** — ransom insular abnormal solarium alumni

4) **DESPONDENT** — opened sodden pendent stopped denoted

5) **TREMENDOUS** — roundest endorsed stormed mourned resumed

6) **BREAKTHROUGH** — burger rougher outrage authors harbour

7) **DETERMINATION** — entertained atonement nominated ornamented marionette

8) **UNAVAILABLE** — naive vanilla unveiled liable invaluable

9) **MATERIALISM** — immaterial alarmist elitism maritime simmers

10) **SEPTUGENARIAN** — sergeant praised nursing pageants repeating

3. Mixed Examples

Exercise 11: 4 Complete the crossword by fitting the five words horizontally or vertically into the grid:

Score

1)
	I	
	R	
	E	

BET GET ORE JOB JIG

2)
B	E	E

BEL EEL OWE EWE BOB

3)
I		
L		
L		

LEG LEA NEE NAG INN

4)
T	O	O

ODD ONE AND TAB BED

Underline the one word which cannot be made from the letters of the word in capital letters.

5) **CONTRADICTION** concordant indicator tradition notation contacted

6) **GRANDPARENT** arranged narrated regarded adapter pendant

7) **TRANSFORMATION** rotations martians animator transformer rainstorm

Underline the one word which can be made from the letters of the word in capital letters.

8) **LISTENABLE** televise elbow linseed neither baseline

9) **HIBERNATE** beneath retained nation habitat ebonite

10) **VENTRILOQUIST** versatile intrusive quantity tribute enquiry

Chapter Twelve
WORD MANIPULATION

Word Manipulation involves making a change to a word or words by Adding or Subtracting Letters, Rearranging Letters to make a new word, finding a Rhyming Word or changing one word to another word letter by letter.

1. Adding or Subtracting Letters
a. Type 1 - A List of Words

In this type of question a list of words is provided and the same letter is added, either to the beginning of each word or the end of each word depending on the question.

Example: Which same letter can be added at the beginning of each word to make five new words?

__old   __race   __host   __amble   __loss

1. Quickly examine the words and see if the letter that could be added immediately comes to mind.

2. Work through the letters of the alphabet and try to fit them onto the beginning of the words. For example, is it **a**, then **b**, then **c**, etc.? When we get to **g** we find it can be added to the beginning of every word to make five new words.

      gold   **g**race   **g**host   **g**amble   **g**loss

Answer: The letter **g** will fit onto the beginning of every word in the series.

Exercise 12: 1 Write the letter which will complete all five words:

Score

1) _lake _lag _ate _lair _low   *f*
2) _ale _age _an _air _ace   *p*
3) _hatch _able _oil _race _ear   *t*
4) _void _maze _loft _go _part   *a*
5) _ark _rake _ash _read _aunt   *d*
6) crow_ boar_ grin_ angle_ bran_ *d*
7) line_ bee_ no_ badge_ live_   *r*
8) cut_ sing_ kit_ grip_ stamped_ *e*
9) hone_ arm_ bell_ oil_ all_   *y*
10) den_ sea_ close_ hear_ isle_   ____

b. Type 2 - Adding a Letter

In this form of question, one letter is added to any part of a given word to change it to a new word which corresponds to the meaning given in the clue.

Example: Add one letter to the word in capital letters to make a new word. The meaning of the new word is given in the clue.

EAT: tidy _____

1. Focus on the clue as this usually suggests the answer. The clue 'tidy' means to be neat or orderly. Both meanings are possibilities but **NEAT** looks like the right answer.

2. Check that **NEAT** can be made by adding one letter to **EAT**. An **N** can be added to **EAT** to make **NEAT**.

Answer: **NEAT** means 'tidy'.

Exercise 12: 2

Add one letter to the word in capital letters to form a new word corresponding to the meaning given:

Score

1) **DEAD**: anticipate with fear _____ R
2) **LANE**: a flat surface _____ P
3) **RANGE**: a fruit _____ O
4) **SING**: a flexible strap _____ T
5) **WHIT**: a colour _____ E
6) **OWL**: poultry _____ F
7) **RESTATING**: beginning again _____ R
8) **TAPING**: knocking _____ P
9) **FLED**: put in place _____ I
10) **BRIDE**: over an obstacle _____ G

c. Type 3 - Subtracting a Letter

In this form of question, one letter is subtracted from any part of a given word to change it to a new word which corresponds to the meaning given in the clue.

Example: Subtract one letter from the word in capital letters to leave a new word. The meaning of the word is given in the clue.

VICE: frozen water _____

1. Focus on the clue as this usually suggests the answer. The clue 'frozen water' means a form of ice. When water is frozen it turns into **ICE**.

2. Check that **ICE** can be made by subtracting the **V** from **VICE**.

Answer: **ICE** means 'frozen water'.

Exercise 12: 3

Remove one letter from the word in capital letters to form a new word corresponding to the meaning given:

1) **WANT**: an insect — ANT
2) **DWELL**: source of water — WELL
3) **GROUT**: a disease — GOUT
4) **GRATE**: a fixed price — RATE
5) **FACT**: to do something — ACT
6) **COMPLETE**: strive to win — COMPETE
7) **TRIPE**: ready to eat — RIPE
8) **HEDGE**: outside limit — EDGE
9) **WAIVING**: a form of greeting — WAVING
10) **STRAINER**: soft sports shoe — TRAINER

2. Compound Words

A **Compound Word** is formed when two words are joined together to make a new word. The first word is called a **Prefix** and the second word is called a **Suffix**. This type of question relies on recognising at least one or two of the words given in order to answer the question.

a. Prefix

Example: Write the word that can be added to each of the following words to make new compound words.

___science   ___firm   ___dense
___text   ___cave

1. Examine each word in turn as it may prompt the correct prefix. It is best to focus on the easier words, as some are more difficult to recognise. The prefix **con** will fit with the options ___**firm** and ___**text**. To **confirm** is to establish the truth or correctness of something and **context** refers to the parts of something written or spoken that immediately precede and follow a word or passage and clarify its meaning.

2. Check that **con** works with the remaining options. It seems to fit as:

   conscience refers to a person's inner understanding of right and wrong.

   condense means to make something denser or more concentrated.

   concave means curving in or hollowed inward.

   Answer: The prefix **con** can be placed in front of each of the words.

Exercise 12: 4 Write the word that can be added to each of the following words to make new compound words:

Score

1) ___natural   ___glue   ___market
   ___charge   ___star   _____

2) ___ordinary   ___terrestrial   ___position
   ___judicial   ___mural   _____

3) ___bid   ___mat   ___ever
   ___got   ___age   _____

4) ___stone   ___paper   ___blast
   ___storm   ___bank   _____

5) ___hole   ___able   ___ray
   ___folio   ___age   _____

6) ___side   ___fit   ___burst
   ___line   ___put   _____

7) ___able   ___ion   ___ate
   ___arise   ___ice   _____

8) ___tend   ___come   ___active
   ___put   ___vest   _____

9) ___violet   ___modern   ___sound
   ___marine   ___microscopic   _____

10) ___go   ___dog   ___stand
    ___cover   ___take   _____

b. Suffix

Example: Write the word that can be placed at the end of each of the following words to make new compound words.

just___   corn___   not___
coward___   off___

1. Examine each word in turn as it may prompt the correct suffix. Again, it is best to focus on the easier words, as some are more difficult to recognise. The suffix **ice** will fit with the options **just___** and **off___**. **Justice** is the meting out of deserved punishment or reward and an **office** is a room used for administration and business.

2. Check that **ice** works with the remaining options. It seems to fit as:

   cornice is a decorative plaster moulding on a building.

   notice means to observe or pay attention to something.

   cowardice is a lack of courage in facing danger.

Answer: The suffix **ice** should be placed after each of the words.

Exercise 12: 5

Write the word that can be placed at the end of each of the following words to make new compound words:

1) mass___   band___   line___
   ramp___   host___   _____

2) child___   neighbour___   brother___
   knight___   adult___   _____

3) ham___   brace___   tab___
   eye___   scar___   _____

4) home___   for___   to___
   after___   back___   _____

5) friend___   citizen___   member___
   battle___   flag___   _____

6) other___   length___   clock___
   like___   width___   _____

7) port___   comfort___   accept___
   honour___   breath___   _____

8) awe___   whole___   flavour___
   tire___   hand___   _____

9) invent___   man___   act___
   do___   edit___   _____

10) under___   a___   half___
    run___   stair___   _____

3. Two Missing Letters

In Workbook 1 this question type occurs but only one letter is missing between two words. E.g. What letter completes both words?

THOUGH (__) ROUT

This is best solved by trying out letters of the alphabet in the space. Is it **A**? Is it **B**? etc.

The letter that fits is **T**: **THOUGH (T) ROUT**

This gives the words **THOUGHT** and **TROUT**.

The question becomes more difficult if there are **Two Missing Letters** but the same basic approach can be used.

Example: Write the two missing letters which will end the first word and start the second word.

BISCU (__) CHY

1. Study the two words carefully and see if the clues have triggered the correct answer. There are not many words that begin with **BISCU** so the word **BISCUIT** may suggest itself and this is the correct answer. If this approach does not work, then move to step 2.

2. Try out the letters of the alphabet in the first space since placing one correct letter in the space may prompt the correct answer. If the letter **I** is selected, **BISCU** becomes **BISCUI** and this should suggest the second letter is **T**.

BISCU (IT) CHY

Answer: The two missing letters are **I** and **T**.
(The completed words are **biscuit** and **itchy**.)

Exercise 12: 6 Write the two letters which will end the first word and start the second word:

Score

1) ANG (___) VEL   2) RESEMB (___) MONADE

3) PET (___) ONG   4) SHUTT (___) ISURE

5) DELE (___) APOT   6) WELCO (___) MBERS

7) ORPH (___) CHOR   8) ROOMMA (___) ENAGER

9) BAS (___) ING   10) FINALI (___) NSIBLE

4. Word Chains

Word Chains occur in two forms, both of which require basic spelling skills combined with a simple technique.

a. Type 1

Example: Change the first word into the last word by changing one letter at a time and making a new, different word in the middle.

SAND _____ **HARD**

1. Write the words in list form as follows and fill in the letters that will remain constant and not change. These have been emboldened and placed in the middle row.

   S **A** N D
   _ **A** _ D
   H **A** R D

   Try out the two possibilities in the remaining spaces:

   S A N D
   ↓
   S A R D
   ↑
   H A R D

   If the **S** from **SAND** is used in the first space, then the **R** from **HARD** must be used in the second space. This produces **SARD**, which is not a word. This means the other combination must give the correct answer.

   S A N D
   ↓
   H A N D
   ↑
   H A R D

   If the **N** from **SAND** is placed in the second space, then the **H** from **HARD** must be placed in the first space and this will give **HAND**, which is a word.

   Answer: **HAND** is the middle word.

Exercise 12: 7 — Change the first word into the last word by changing one letter at a time and making a new, different word in the middle:

1) **CHIN** _____ **SPIN**

2) **DIAL** _____ **DEAF**

3) **TOWN** _____ **DAWN**

4) **CALF** _____ **TALL**

5) **MIME** _____ **LIVE**

6) **SAVED** _____ **WAXED**

7) **WHINE** _____ **WRITE**

8) **FARCE** _____ **FORTE**

9) **OASIS** _____ **BASIC**

10) **ALONE** _____ **AMONG**

Score

b. Type 2

The same basic Word Chains technique is used for the second question type and it is repeated.

Example: Change the first word into the last word by changing one letter at a time and making two new, different words in the middle.

FIND _____ _____ WILL

1. Write the words in list form as follows and fill in the letter that will remain constant (does not change). This letter has been emboldened and placed in the two spaces.

42 © 2015 Stephen Curran

```
    F I N D
    _ I _ _
    _ I _ _
    W I L L
```

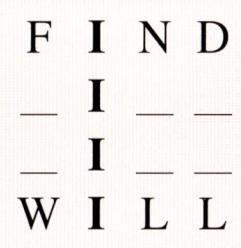

2. Try out the three possibilities. We can ignore the third word for the moment. One combination is as follows:

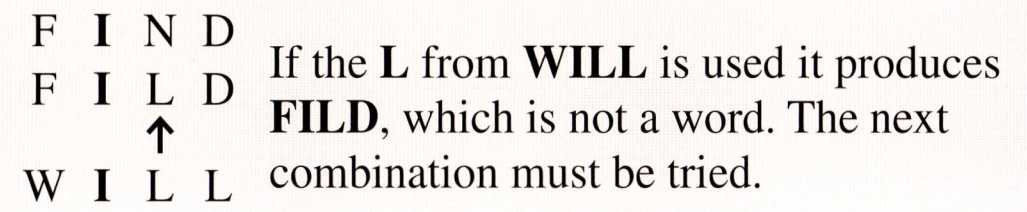

```
F I N D
F I L D
    ↑
W I L L
```
If the **L** from **WILL** is used it produces **FILD**, which is not a word. The next combination must be tried.

```
F I N D
F I N L
      ↑
W I L L
```
If the other **L** from **WILL** is used it produces **FINL**, which is not a word either. The final combination is:

```
F I N D
W I N D
↑
W I L L
```

If we use the **W** from **WILL** this will produce **WIND**, which is the correct word.

3. Now fill in the letters that remain constant (do not change). These letters have been placed in the two middle rows.

```
F I N D
W I N D
W I _ _
W I L L
```

4. Try out the two possibilities. One combination is as follows:

```
W I N D
  ↓
W I N L
      ↑
W I L L
```
If the second **L** from **WILL** is used in the last space, then the **N** from **WIND** must be used in the third space. This produces **WINL**, which is not a word. This means

the other combination must give the correct answer.

```
W  I  N  D
      ↓
W  I  L  D
      ↑
W  I  L  L
```

If the **L** from **WILL** is placed in the third space, then the **D** from **WIND** must be placed in the last space and this will give **WILD**, which is a word.

The completed list of words is as follows:

F I N D
W I N D
W I L D
W I L L

Answer: The two missing words are **WIND** and **WILD**.

Exercise 12: 8

Change the first word into the last word by changing one letter at a time and making two new, different words in the middle:

1) **JAWS** _____ _____ **EARL**

2) **WARD** _____ _____ **FORK**

3) **DEBT** _____ _____ **LIFT**

4) **PLAIT** _____ _____ **BLANK**

5) **DRAIN** _____ _____ **BRAND**

6) **THUMB** _____ _____ **TRAMP**

7) **ROGUE** _____ _____ **VALUE**

8) **ROAD** _____ _____ **HOLD**

9) **PORE** _____ _____ **LARK**

10) **COVER** _____ _____ **POSER**

Score

5. Rearranging Letters

Rearranging Letters questions occur in two forms. Either an **Anagram** of the given word must be found (another word made from an existing word) or a word must be made from some **Jumbled Letters**. A clue is usually given and this makes the task easier. Shorter words are easy to find but many letter combinations can be created from longer words and this makes the task much harder.

a. Anagrams

Example: Rearrange the letters of the word in capitals to form a word corresponding to the meaning given.

BRAG: grasp suddenly   _____

1. Focus on the clue as this may suggest the word immediately. To 'grasp suddenly' suggests a number of words like **seize**, **snatch** and **clutch** but these all have five or six letters and do not fit. Four-letter words like **GRIP** or **GRAB** are also possible. Only the **G** and the **R** in **GRIP** fit so the correct answer must be **GRAB**. If step 1 does not work then move on to step 2.

2. Write the letters either jumbled up or in a circle as this can help trigger the answer.

   G B
   A R

   If step 2 does not work move on to step 3.

3. Consider the various combinations of letters, a four-letter word creates 24 different combinations. The best approach is to identify two-letter combinations that could begin the word and might suggest the answer. For example:

   BR BA AB AR AG RA GA GR

Answer: **GRAB** means to 'grasp suddenly' and is an anagram of **BRAG**.

Exercise 12: 9

Rearrange the letters of the word in capital letters to form a word corresponding to the meaning given:

Score

1) **AGREES**: oily substance _____

2) **METEOR**: far away _____

3) **DASHED**: sheltered from light _____

4) **CAUSES**: liquids served with food _____

5) **BURNED**: a heavy load _____

6) **SEASIDE**: illness _____

7) **MOBBING**: dropping an explosive _____

8) **SECURED**: saved _____

9) **LICENSE**: absence of sound _____

10) **INFRINGE**: removing impurities _____

b. Jumbled Letters

Example: Rearrange the capital letters to form a word corresponding to the meaning given.
RUDAG: watch over _____

The same approach is used for Anagrams and Jumbled Letters.

1. Focus on the clue as this may suggest the word immediately. To 'watch over' suggests a number of words like **protect**, **safeguard**, **defend** and **shield** but

these all have six letters or more and do not fit. If step 1 does not work move on to step 2.

2. Write the letters either jumbled up or in a circle as this can help trigger the answer.

```
     R    U              R
  A    D    G         G     U
                     A   D
```

If step 2 does not work move on to step 3.

3. Writing out all the letter combinations for five letters is far more difficult as it presents many more possibilities. However, identifying two-letter combinations that could begin the word might suggest the answer:

DR   RA   AR   DA   GR   GU

4. Think again about the clue and of any words that might begin with these letters. **GU** should trigger the word **GUARD** and this looks correct.

5. Check that the letters of **GUARD** match the Jumbled Letters **RUDAG**.

Answer: **GUARD** means 'watch over' and it can be made from **RUDAG**.

Exercise 12: 10

Rearrange the letters in capitals to form a word corresponding to the meaning given:

1) **IEDDVI**:   separated into parts   _____

2) **EGCNYT**:   a young swan   _____

3) **TTPIEE**:   small and dainty   _____

4) **RAHUOT**: a writer _____

5) **TEILOSH**: showing dislike _____

6) **SEENDDC**: move downwards _____

7) **BALUVALE**: worth a lot of money _____

8) **BENSSEIL**: showing common sense _____

9) **NADDOBANE**: deserted _____

10) **USAWOEHER**: storeroom _____

6. Rhyming Words

Rhyming Words involves finding a word that rhymes with another word by using either a given word definition or a contextual clue. The word that must be found rarely follows the same spelling pattern as the given word.

a. Type 1

Example: Insert the word that will complete the sentence and rhymes with the word in capital letters.

HEIGHT: The _____ string got caught in a tree.

1. Focus on the sentence. Ask yourself what could get caught up in a tree. It is obviously a type of object that can fly.

2. Think about things that can fly that also rhyme with

'height.' This will more than likely trigger the correct answer of 'kite.'

Answer: **Kite** rhymes with **HEIGHT**.

Exercise 12: 11a

Insert the word that will complete the sentence and rhymes with the word in capital letters:

Score

1) **LIMB**: He went to the _____ every evening after work to stay fit.

2) **OFF**: The common cold is often accompanied by a _____ .

3) **TREE**: The firemen worked hard to clear the _____ from the car accident.

4) **ROUGH**: Whilst carrying the sofa downstairs they left _____ marks on the walls.

5) **BEAU**: I need thread to _____ on this button.

b. Type 2

Example: Write the word that rhymes with the word in capital letters and corresponds to the meaning given.

TOWEL: A sound made by a hostile animal

1. Focus on the clue. Ask yourself what king of sounds a hostile or aggressive animal might make.
2. Think about sounds that hostile animals make that rhyme with 'towel.' This will more than likely suggest the

correct answer of 'growl.'
Answer: **Growl** rhymes with **TOWEL**.

Exercise 12: 11b Write the word that rhymes with the word in capital letters and corresponds to the meaning given:

6) **BLUE**: In accordance with fact _____

7) **FLEW**: An adhesive substance _____

8) **GREED**: To come before something _____

9) **FOUR**: To make a hole with a tool _____

10) **PAY**: An arranged bunch of flowers _____

7. Mixed Examples

Exercise 12: 12 Answer the following questions:

Write the letter which will complete all five words below:

1) _eight   _hole   _ash   _ring   _heel   _____

Add one letter to the word in capital letters to form a new word corresponding to the meaning given:

2) **RATIO**:   limit the supply   _____

Remove one letter from the word in capital letters to form a new word corresponding to the meaning given:

3) **STARTLING**:   a songbird   _____

Write the word that can be put in front of each of the following words to make new compound words:

4) ___man   ___card   ___age   ___script   ___box   _____

Write the word that can be put at the end of each of the following words to make new compound words:

5) emotion___   age___   care___   flaw___   blame___   _____

Write the two letters which will end the first word and start the second word:

6) **MARI** (____) **ARBY**   _____

7) **CUCUMB** (____) **UPTION**   _____

Change the first word into the last word by changing one letter at a time and making two new, different words in the middle:

8) **GLOW**   _____   _____   **SHOE**

Rearrange the letters in capitals to form a word corresponding to the meaning given:

9) **MESLIAS**:   without purpose   _____

Rearrange the letters of the word in capital letters to form a word corresponding to the meaning given:

10) **SALESMEN**: without a title   _____

Score

Chapter Thirteen
GROUPING
1. Identifying the Group

Grouping involves sorting words into specific categories. It can also be called word taxonomy. Some forms of this question type have been covered in Workbook 3 under Classification. It draws upon a broad knowledge of the meanings of words and how they relate to other words.

a. Single Grouping

Example: There is a connection between the three words on the outside of the brackets and two of the words inside the brackets.

Underline the two words:

PIECE   SECTION   PART
(full, fragment, circle, whole, portion)

1. Identify the overall grouping of the given words. The words **PIECE**, **SECTION** and **PART** describe an amount or quantity that is a share or fraction of a total.

2. Now look for words that fit this definition. The words **full**, **whole** and **circle** are incorrect as they refer to something complete. This leaves only **fragment** and **portion**, which both mean a part of something bigger.

Answer: The two connected words are **fragment** and **portion**.

Exercise 13: 1

There is a connection between the three words on the outside of the brackets and two of the words inside the brackets. Underline the two words:

1) **MILK   JUICE   WATER**
(butter, tea, sugar, petrol, eggs)

2) **RHYTHM   METRE   PULSE**
(kilometre, rhyme, heart, beat, tempo)

3) **HOLLER   YELL   SHRIEK**
(scream, cry, whisper, talk, discuss)

4) **TSUNAMI   FLOOD   TORRENT**
(tap, wave, hosepipe, deluge, hurricane)

5) **CURL   RINGLET   COIL**
(bow, spiral, crease, whorl, hair)

6) **TRUMPET   CORNET   TROMBONE**
(horn, tuba, violin, cone, triangle)

7) **FLINT   GRANITE   MARBLE**
(chalk, worktop, tool, counter, slate)

8) **AIM   END   GOAL**
(target, ball, objective, aimless, start)

9) **BASIL   OREGANO   BAY**
(thrive, cove, thyme, time, chive)

10) **TADPOLE   FROG   TOAD**
(moth, salamander, cricket, newt, spider)

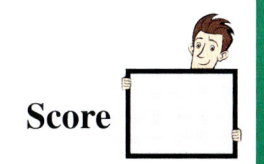

Score

b. Multiple Grouping

Example: Look at these groups of words.

A	B	C	D
lacrosse	barge	tin	ballet
cricket	dinghy	brass	salsa

Choose the correct group for each of the words below. Write in the letter:

gondola ___   hockey ___   waltz ___

1. Identify the overall groupings of the given words. These are:

A	B	C	D
sports	boats	metals	dances

2. Start by grouping the easy words. For example, **hockey** is a sport and therefore belongs in group **A**.

3. Now look at the harder words. A **waltz** is a type of dance and belongs in group **D**. A **gondola** is a kind of boat and belongs in group **B**.

Answer: **gondola – B, hockey – A, waltz – D**

Exercise 13: 2 Choose the correct group for each of the words below. Write in the letter:

A	B	C	D
June	robin	paint	beret
October	mockingbird	chalk	cap

1) crow ___   fez ___   watercolour ___

2) chaffinch ___   boater ___   April ___

3) blackbird ___	January ___	charcoal ___
4) sparrow ___	deerstalker ___	pastel ___
5) August ___	sombrero ___	ink ___

A	B	C	D
French	tiger	violin	oak
British	puma	timpani	pine

6) elm ___	Russian ___	jaguar ___
7) cello ___	cheetah ___	willow ___
8) Thai ___	beech ___	tuba ___
9) oboe ___	cougar ___	ash ___
10) juniper ___	bassoon ___	Canadian ___

2. Size, Sequence or Position

This is a type of Grouping where objects are categorised by **Size** (how big they are in relation to other objects), **Sequence** (in which order they should be placed numerically) or **Position** (how they should be ranked by level of importance).

Example: Underline the word that would come in the middle if the following were put in order of size, sequence or position:

adult   child   pensioner   baby   teenager

1. Identify whether the grouping is by size, sequence or position. This particular grouping is status and age of human beings so it covers two categories. Age relates

to sequence (numerical) and status refers to position (ranking).

2. We can use both grouping types to order the words. Start with the youngest and the lowest in status (**baby**) and work through to the highest.

baby   child   teenager   adult   pensioner

3. Now select the third word in the grouping, which will be **teenager**.

Answer: The middle word is **teenager**.

Exercise 13: 3

Underline the word that would come in the middle if the following were put in order of size, sequence or position:

1) metre   kilometre   centimetre   foot   millimetre

2) Earth   Venus   Mars   Mercury   Jupiter

3) starling   swan   eagle   ostrich   duck

4) sea   stream   brook   ocean   river

5) sun   blizzard   snow   cloud   rain

6) rowboat   ferry   kayak   motorboat   barge

7) letter   word   paragraph   sentence   syllable

8) county   village   city   country   town

9) leaf   petal   bud   root   stem

10) cotton   cloth   plant   yarn   garment

Score

3. Mixed Examples

Exercise 13: 4 Answer the following questions:

There is a connection between the three words on the outside of the brackets and two of the words inside the brackets. Underline the two words:

1) **PARASITE   SCROUNGER   FREELOADER**
   (bug, hinder, pest, sponge, allow)

2) **GALAXY   ASTEROID   METEOR**
   (comet, lion, asterisk, universe, rock)

3) **RETRIEVER   CORGI   GREYHOUND**
   (beagle, blackbird, Siamese, bugle, whippet)

4) **JUG   BEAKER   FLASK**
   (coal, casket, canteen, carafe, chest)

Choose the correct group for each of the words below. Write in the letter:

A	B	C	D
carrot	father	rose	ant
marrow	aunt	daisy	dragonfly

5) carnation ___   sprout ___   uncle ___

6) cricket ___   cousin ___   peony ___

7) radish ___   moth ___   tulip ___

8) leek ___   beetle ___   niece ___

Underline the word that would come in the middle if the following were put in order of size, sequence or position:

9) least   many   few   none   most

10) goat   horse   sheep   chicken   cow

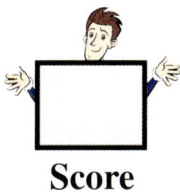

Score

Chapter Fourteen
REVISION
1. Alphabet Work

A B C D E F G H I J K L M N O P Q R S T U V W X Y Z

Exercise 14: 1   Answer the following questions:

1) Write these words in alphabetical order:

   knives   knight   known   knitting   kneecap

   _____ _____ _____ _____ _____

2) Underline the word which would come last if these words were placed in alphabetical order:

   orderly   ordinary   ordeal   orbital   order

3) Underline the word which would come fourth if these words were written backwards and then arranged in alphabetical order:

   annually   initially   vitally   ally   really

4) Underline the word which would come third if these words were written backwards and then arranged in alphabetical order:

   asteroid   cuboid   android   devoid   avoid

Use the alphabet above to help with the following questions:

5) How many more consonants are in the word **DISAPPOINTMENT** than vowels?   _____

6) Which letter appears most often in the word **SENSATIONALISM**?   _____

A B C D E F G H I J K L M N O P Q R S T U V W X Y Z

7) Make a word of three letters from the letters which appear more than once in the word **TOOTHACHE**. _____

8) Which word would come second if these word were written backwards and the arranged in alphabetical order:

   anxious   obvious   devious   victorious   conscious

9) Which letter appears most often in the word **DISAPPEARANCE**? _____

10) Make a word of four letters from the letters which appear more than once in the word **UNINTELLIGIBLE**. _____

Score

2. More Codes

A B C D E F G H I J K L M N O P Q R S T U V W X Y Z

Exercise 14: 2a Answer the following questions:

1) The code **ZGHBXP** stands for **BOILED** and **RONJGD** stands for **MASCOT**.
   a) What does **JOBRXND** stand for? _____
   b) What is the code for **DECIMAL**? _____

2) If **472638** stands for **SPINAL**, what does **783264** stand for? _____

3) If **£*!@%#** stands for **RENTAL**, what does **#*%£!@** stand for? _____

4) If **TEARFUL** in code is **22 B 3 O 8 R 14**, what is **JUSTICE** in the same code? _____

5) If **PPOUNMMP** stands for **PUMP** then **PURE** is written _____ .

3. Word Play

Exercise 14: 2b Answer the following questions:

Complete each crossword by fitting the five words horizontally or vertically into the grid:

6) | A | D | D |
   |---|---|---|
   | | | |
   | | | |

DOT
AWN
WOO
NET
DOE

7) | A | C | E |
   |---|---|---|
   | | | |
   | | | |

COW
TOY
EWE
ATE
EYE

Underline the one word which cannot be made from the letters of the word in capital letters:

8) **DICTIONARIES**   indicators   canister   scorned   trainers   discretion

Underline the one word which can be made from the letters of the word in capital letters:

9) **GEOGRAPHICAL**   grill   ripen   hoard   poached   aerial

10) **ENJAMBMENT**   amend   neaten   abate   bantam   emenate

Score

4. Word Manipulation

Exercise 14: 3 Answer the following questions:

Write the letter which will complete all five words below:

1) __go   __mail   __state   __vent   __late   ____

2) media__   law__   sire__   woke__   brow__   ____

Add one letter to the word in capitals to form a new word corresponding to the meaning given:

3) **EIGHT**: a vertical measurement _____

Remove one letter from the word in capitals to form a new word corresponding to the meaning given:

4) **TRANCE**: to discover by investigation _____

Write the two letters, which will end the first word and start the second word:

5) **SQUEL** (____) **RONICLE** _____

Rearrange the letters in capitals to form a word corresponding to the meaning given:

6) **ROUNEVS**: Anxious _____

7) **RENTALS**: Adult deer horns _____

Turn the first word into the last word by changing one letter at a time and making two new different words in the middle:

8) **TUNA** _____ _____ **ZONE**

Write the word that can be put in front of each of the following words to make new compound words:

9) ___letter   ___worthy   ___print   ___reel   ___paper _____

Write the word that can be put at the end of each of the following words to make new compound words:

10) life___   a___   child___   dream___   lady___ _____

Score

5. Grouping

Exercise 14: 4 Answer the following questions:

Choose the correct group for each of the words below. Write in the letter:

Score

A	B	C	D
Bamboo	Needle	Jade	Asteroid
Nettle	Seam	Olive	Comet

1) Thimble ___   Meteor ___   Thistle ___
2) Emerald ___   Clover ___   Hem ___
3) Star ___   Pin ___   Lime ___

A	B	C	D
Anger	Lotus	Badget	Mustard
Disgust	Heather	Stoat	Honey

4) Banana ___   Rose ___   Squirrel ___
5) Lavender ___ Weasel ___   Fear ___
6) Love ___   Ochre ___   Snowdrop ___

There is a connection between the three words on the outside of the brackets and two of the words inside the brackets. Underline the two words:

7) **SHAME   DISGRACE   DISHONOUR**

   (strain, stigma, stain, segment, sentry)

8) **KESTREL   KITE   FALCON**

   (buzzer, prey, hawk, duck, eagle)

Underline the word that would come in the middle if the following were put in order of size, sequence or position:

9) run   walk   sprint   jog   amble

10) ten   thousand   unit   million   hundred

Answers

11+ Verbal Reasoning Year 5-7 GL & Other Styles Workbook 3

Chapter Nine
Alphabet Work

Exercise 9: 1
1) butter, drawn, indigo, mutton, uncle
2) density, dentist, elastic, elbow, elect
3) sand, sandal, sandbag, sandbank, sandstone
4) cataclysm, catacomb, catapult, category, cater
5) transcribe, transcript, translate, transmit, transpire
6) illegal, illiterate, illuminate, illumination, illustration
7) encampment, encase, encourage, encrypt, encyclopaedia
8) prolific, prominent, promotion, propaganda, prosper
9) whoever, wholesale, wholesome, whomever, whosoever
10) quicken, quicksand, quilting, quinoa, quintet

Exercise 9: 2a
1) lashing
2) barracuda
3) hearth
4) pronate
5) roughage

Exercise 9: 2b
6) spoilt
7) seawater
8) cleansing
9) thorough
10) clamber

Exercise 9: 3
1) W 2) V
3) E 4) 3
5) 1 6) E
7) TIE 8) LMNOP
9) 11th 10) SIN

Exercise 9: 4
1) rapport, recipient, rhetorical, rotate, rummage
2) gender, general, generic, genetics, genius
3) question
4) transformation
5) sentence
6) dedication
7) T
8) 4
9) ABCDE
10) O

Chapter Ten
More Codes

Exercise 10: 1
1) THING
2) LEARNT
3) AXYHRJ
4) DESPAIR
5) FZDAPQEK
6) a) MONTH
   b) UZPS
7) a) EDUCATIVE
   b) XYYOGSK
8) a) SEBACEOUS
   b) IDZGQGJ
9) a) MANHOLE
   b) XPBQX
10) a) HOMONYM
    b) CPCHVCJ

Exercise 10: 2a
1) BRIEF
2) 46219
3) BRAVED
4) 9425376
5) CHARMING

Exercise 10: 2b
6) a) OCEAN
   b) £*%
7) a) MARCH
   b) $%!
8) a) NEARER
   b) ?#£
9) a) DOES
   b) %$&£#?
10) a) ACROSS
    b) $@%&

Exercise 10: 3a
1) ARC
2) EVEN
3) 11 16 5 21
4) JUICY
5) 22 13 6 25 1

Exercise 10: 3b
6) 23 P 6 G 20
7) TIGER
8) 13 C 17 X 10 U
9) RUFFLED
10) P 24 Z 13 P 22 J

Exercise 10: 4
1) ANT
2) LOOP

11+ Verbal Reasoning Year 5-7 GL & Other Styles Workbook 3

Answers

3) CZOYIXNW
4) SOW
5) STIJNOKL
6) NONE
7) PPAGGE
8) EXTRA
9) SMALL
10) IQMRASGTE

Exercise 10: 5
1) a) CANAPE
   b) OIIOIIPJ
2) FITNESS
3) IAXLFVD
4) AGREES
5) 849285
6) a) REVEAL
   b) +%£#&
7) EXIST
8) 13 15 4 9 6 25
9) RING
10) ZSYCXRWAVPU

Chapter Eleven
Word Play
Exercise 11: 1

1)
B	O	W
I	R	E
N	E	T

2)
C	R	Y
A	Y	E
T	E	N

3)
D	A	M
O	D	E
E	O	N

4)
F	I	G
I	C	Y
R	E	M

5)
O	A	K
U	S	E
T	H	Y

6)
P	A	N
E	V	E
W	E	T

7)
Y	A	M
E	R	A
S	K	Y

8)
H	I	T
A	C	E
S	E	E

9)
L	E	D
A	G	A
G	O	D

10)
D	I	M
Y	O	U
E	N	D

Exercise 11: 2
1) tourist
2) disable
3) politician
4) aeronauts
5) trainers
6) tongue
7) violent
8) mound
9) lurked
10) asthma

Exercise 11: 3
1) shortest
2) spiders
3) abnormal
4) stopped
5) endorsed
6) authors
7) entertained
8) unveiled
9) simmers
10) praised

Exercise 11: 4

1)
J	I	G
O	R	E
B	E	T

2)
B	E	E
O	W	E
B	E	L

3)
I	N	N
L	E	A
L	E	G

4)
T	O	O
A	N	D
B	E	D

5) contacted
6) regarded
7) transformer
8) baseline
9) beneath
10) intrusive

© 2015 Stephen Curran

Answers

Chapter Twelve
Word Manipulation

Exercise 12: 1
1) f   2) p
3) t   4) a
5) d   6) d
7) r   8) e
9) y   10) t

Exercise 12: 2
1) DREAD
2) PLANE
3) ORANGE
4) SLING
5) WHITE
6) FOWL
7) RESTARTING
8) TAPPING
9) FILED
10) BRIDGE

Exercise 12: 3
1) ANT
2) WELL
3) GOUT
4) RATE
5) ACT
6) COMPETE
7) RIPE
8) EDGE
9) WAVING
10) TRAINER

Exercise 12: 4
1) super
2) extra
3) for
4) sand
5) port
6) out
7) not
8) in
9) ultra
10) under

Exercise 12: 5
1) age
2) hood
3) let
4) ward
5) ship
6) wise
7) able
8) some
9) or
10) way

Exercise 12: 6
1) LE   2) LE
3) AL   4) LE
5) TE   6) ME
7) AN   8) TE
9) IC   10) SE

Exercise 12: 7
1) SHIN
2) DEAL
3) DOWN
4) CALL
5) LIME
6) WAVED
7) WHITE
8) FORCE
9) BASIS
10) ALONG

Exercise 12: 8
1) JARS EARS
2) WORD WORK
3) DEFT LEFT
4) PLANT PLANK
5) BRAIN BRAID
6) THUMP TRUMP
7) VOGUE VAGUE
8) TOAD TOLD
9) PORK PARK
10) COWER POWER

Exercise 12: 9
1) GREASE
2) REMOTE
3) SHADED
4) SAUCES
5) BURDEN
6) DISEASE
7) BOMBING
8) RESCUED
9) SILENCE
10) REFINING

Exercise 12: 10
1) DIVIDE
2) CYGNET
3) PETITE
4) AUTHOR
5) HOSTILE
6) DESCEND
7) VALUABLE
8) SENSIBLE
9) ABANDONED
10) WAREHOUSE

Exercise 12: 11a
1) gym
2) cough
3) debris
4) scuff
5) sew

Exercise 12: 11b
6) true
7) glue
8) precede
9) bore
10) bouquet

11+ Verbal Reasoning Year 5-7 GL & Other Styles Workbook 3

Answers

Exercise 12: 12
1) W
2) RATION
3) STARLING
4) post
5) less
6) NE
7) ER
8) SLOW SHOW
9) AIMLESS
10) NAMELESS

Chapter Thirteen
Grouping
Exercise 13: 1
1) tea, petrol
2) beat, tempo
3) scream, cry
4) wave, deluge
5) spiral, whorl
6) horn, tuba
7) chalk, slate
8) target, objective
9) thyme, chive
10) salamander, newt

Exercise 13: 2
1) B, D, C
2) B, D, A
3) B, A, C
4) B, D, C
5) A, D, C
6) D, A, B
7) C, B, D
8) A, D, C
9) C, B, D
10) D, C, A

Exercise 13: 3
1) foot
2) Earth
3) eagle
4) river
5) rain
6) motorboat
7) word
8) city
9) leaf
10) yarn

Exercise 13: 4
1) pest, sponge
2) comet, universe
3) beagle, whippet
4) canteen, carafe
5) C, A, B
6) D, B, C
7) A, D, C
8) A, D, B
9) few
10) sheep

Chapter Fourteen
Revision
Exercise 14: 1
1) kneecap, knight, knitting, knives, known
2) ordinary
3) vitally
4) asteroid
5) 4
6) S
7) HOT
8) victorious
9) A
10) LINE

Exercise 14: 2a
1) a) CALMEST
   b) PXJHROB
2) PLAINS
3) LEARNT
4) 12 R 21 Q 11 Z 7
5) PPOUNRME

Exercise 14: 2b

6)
A	D	D
W	O	O
N	E	T

7)
A	C	E
T	O	Y
E	W	E

8) trainers
9) aerial
10) neaten

Exercise 14: 3
1) e
2) n
3) HEIGHT
4) TRACE
5) CH
6) NERVOUS
7) ANTLERS
8) TUNE, TONE
9) news
10) like

Exercise 14: 4
1) B, D, A
2) C, A, B
3) D, B, C
4) D, B, C
5) B, C, A
6) A, D, B
7) stigma, stain
8) hawk, eagle
9) jog
10) hundred

PROGRESS CHARTS

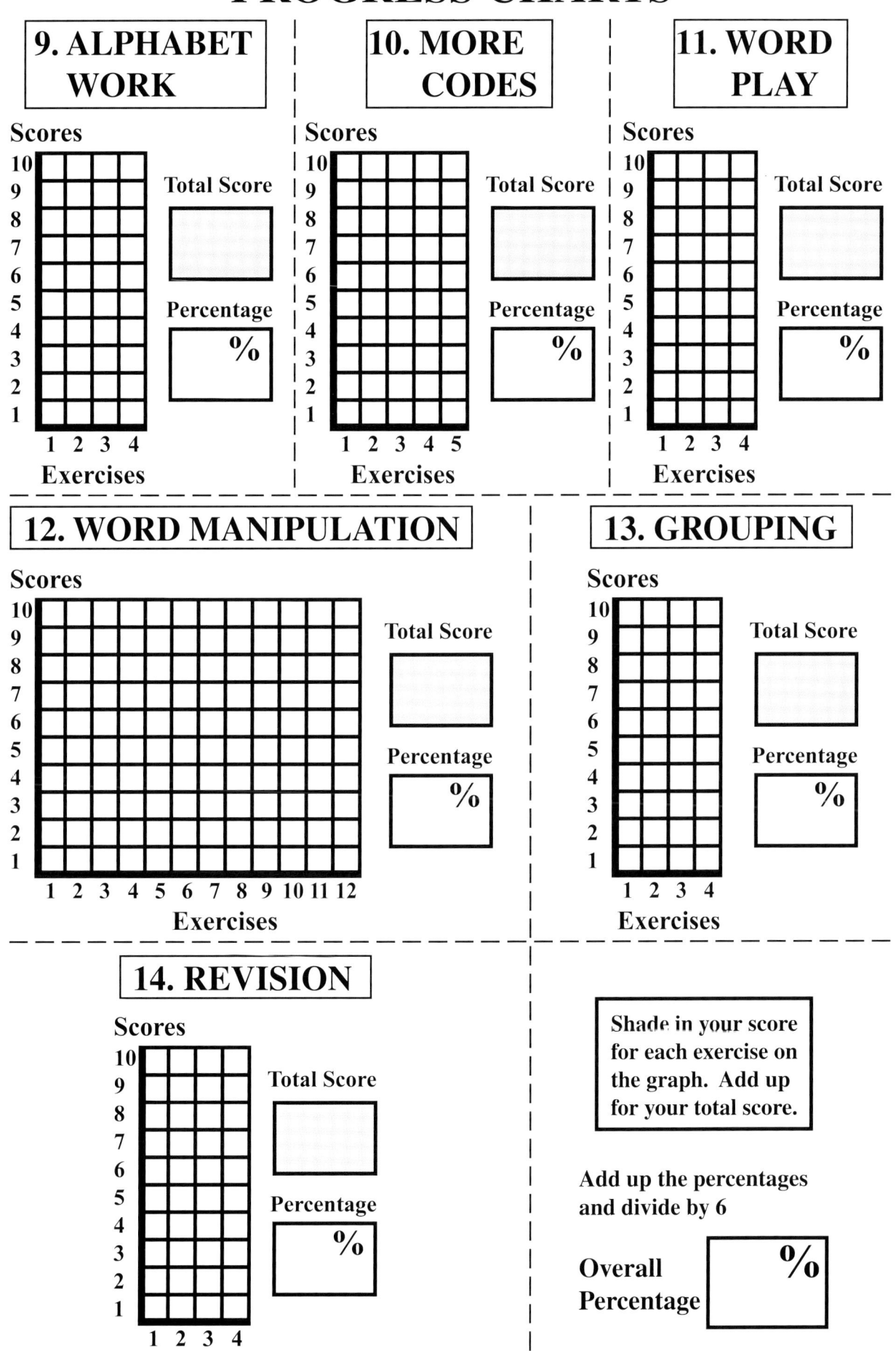

9. ALPHABET WORK
Scores / Exercises 1-4
Total Score
Percentage %

10. MORE CODES
Scores / Exercises 1-5
Total Score
Percentage %

11. WORD PLAY
Scores / Exercises 1-4
Total Score
Percentage %

12. WORD MANIPULATION
Scores / Exercises 1-12
Total Score
Percentage %

13. GROUPING
Scores / Exercises 1-4
Total Score
Percentage %

14. REVISION
Scores / Exercises 1-4
Total Score
Percentage %

Shade in your score for each exercise on the graph. Add up for your total score.

Add up the percentages and divide by 6

Overall Percentage %

© 2015 Stephen Curran

CERTIFICATE OF

ACHIEVEMENT

This certifies

_____

has successfully completed

11+ Verbal Reasoning
Year 5-7 GL & Other Styles
WORKBOOK 3

Overall percentage score achieved [   ] %

Comment _____

_____

Signed _____
(teacher/parent/guardian)

Date _____

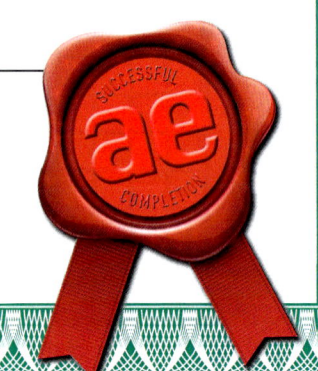